HOW AWESOME CAN YOU BE?

BE A GOOD CITIZEN

by Emma Carlson Berne

Consultant: Beth Gambro,
Reading Specialist, Yorkville, Illinois

Minneapolis, Minnesota

Teaching Tips

Before Reading

- Look at the cover of the book. Discuss the picture and the title.
- Ask readers to brainstorm a list of what they already know about being a good citizen. What can they expect to see in this book?
- Go on a picture walk, looking through the pictures to discuss vocabulary and make predictions about the text.

During Reading

- Read for purpose. As they are reading, encourage readers to think about showing good citizenship in their own lives.
- Ask readers to look for the details of the book. What are the specific ways someone can be a good citizen?
- If readers encounter an unknown word, ask them to look at the sounds in the word. Then, ask them to look at the rest of the page. Are there any clues to help them understand?

After Reading

- Encourage readers to pick a buddy and reread the book together.
- Ask readers to name two ways to be a good citizen that are included in the book. Go back and find the pages that tell about these things.
- Ask readers to write or draw something they learned about being a good citizen.

Credits:
Cover and title page, © PEPPERSMINT/Shutterstock; 3, © yalayama/iStock; 5, © FatCamera/iStock; 7, © Studio Romantic/Shutterstock; 9, © SDI Productions/iStock; 10–11, © ArtMarie/iStock; 13, © Halfpoint/iStock; 14–15, © max-kegfire/iStock; 16–17, © ArtMarie/iStock; 19, © Amorn Suriyan/iStock; 20–21, © Chinnapong/iStock; 22TL, © monkeybusinessimages/iStock; 22TR, © monkeybusinessimages/iStock; 22BL, © hoozone/iStock; 22BR, © fstop123/iStock; 23TL, © kali9/iStock; 23TM, © FatCamera/iStock; 23TR, © Rtimages/Shutterstock; 23BL, © Billion Photos/Shutterstock; 23BM, © FluxFactory/iStock; and 23BR, © adamkaz/iStock.

Library of Congress Cataloging-in-Publication Data

Names: Berne, Emma Carlson, 1979- author.
Title: Be a good citizen / by Emma Carlson Berne ; consultant Beth Gambro.
Description: Minneapolis, Minnesota : Bearport Publishing Company, 2023. |
Series: How awesome can you be? | Includes bibliographical references and index.
Identifiers: LCCN 2022031737 (print) | LCCN 2022031738 (ebook) | ISBN 9798885093217 (library binding) | ISBN 9798885094436 (paperback) | ISBN 9798885095587 (ebook)
Subjects: LCSH: Citizenship--United States--Juvenile literature. | Civics--Juvenile literature.
Classification: LCC JK1759 .B44 2023 (print) | LCC JK1759 (ebook) | DDC 323.6/50973--dc23/eng/20220801
LC record available at https://lccn.loc.gov/2022031737
LC ebook record available at https://lccn.loc.gov/2022031738

Copyright © 2023 Bearport Publishing Company. All rights reserved. No part of this publication may be reproduced in whole or in part, stored in any retrieval system, or transmitted in any form or by any means, electronic, mechanical, photocopying, recording, or otherwise, without written permission from the publisher.

For more information, write to Bearport Publishing, 5357 Penn Avenue South, Minneapolis, MN 55419.

Contents

Being an Awesome Citizen...... 4

Showing Citizenship..................... 22

Glossary 23

Index 24

Read More 24

Learn More Online..................... 24

About the Author 24

Being an Awesome Citizen

We are all part of many **communities**.

Our school is a community.

So is the street where we live.

Helping your community is awesome!

Some communities are bigger.

They can be towns and cities.

People in these places are called **citizens**.

A good citizen thinks about everyone in the community.

You can be a good citizen in many ways.

Volunteer to clean up the lunchroom at school.

This helps make a nice place for everyone to eat.

A good citizen may shovel snow off the sidewalk.

You can make your street safe for each person who lives there.

Thanks, citizen!

Sometimes, the community needs a lot of help.

Many people come together.

Working as a team makes it easy to do a big job!

Is your town planting trees at the park?

Grab a shovel.

Start digging!

Everyone works together to make the park pretty.

You are a citizen of your state and country, too.

When you are 18, you can **vote**.

Voting lets you say what you think the community needs.

Even Earth needs awesome citizens.

Protecting the **planet** helps everyone living here.

Pick up **litter** to keep Earth clean.

You can be an awesome citizen.

Thinking of others feels great.

Let's help our communities!

21

Showing Citizenship

Help your school community by planning a playground pickup!

1. Ask your teacher to help you choose a time.

2. Tell everyone at your school about the litter pickup day.

3. Then, make the playground clean so everyone can have fun!

Glossary

citizens people who belong to a group

communities groups of people who have things in common

litter trash that has been left somewhere

planet a large, round object in space

volunteer to offer to work without pay

vote to pick something as a group

Index

communities 4, 6, 12, 17, 20, 22
country 17
litter 18, 22
planet 18
school 4, 8, 22
street 4, 11
volunteer 8
vote 17

Read More

Fretland VanVoorst, Jenny. *I Am a Good Citizen (Character Education).* Minneapolis: Bellwether Media, 2019.

Murray, Julie. *Citizenship (Character Education).* Minneapolis: ABDO Kids, 2020.

Learn More Online

1. Go to **www.factsurfer.com** or scan the QR code below.
2. Enter "**Be a Good Citizen**" into the search box.
3. Click on the cover of this book to see a list of websites.

About the Author

Emma Carlson Berne lives with her family in Cincinnati, Ohio. She loves being a part of her community!